>TOURIST

*GREATER THAN A ~~         ~~KS ARE
   ALSO AVA~~            ~~ND

Gr~~              ~~ourist
    Series
Reviews from Readers

I think the series is wonderful and beneficial for tourists to get information before visiting the city.

-Seckin Zumbul, Izmir Turkey

I am a world traveler who has read many trip guides but this one really made a difference for me. I would call it a heartfelt creation of a local guide expert instead of just a guide.

-Susy, Isla Holbox, Mexico

New to the area like me, this is a must have!

-Joe, Bloomington, USA

This is a good series that gets down to it when looking for things to do at your destination without having to read a novel for just a few ideas.

-Rachel, Monterey, USA

Good information to have to plan my trip to this destination.

-Pennie Farrell, Mexico

Great ideas for a port day.

-Mary Martin USA

Aptly titled, you won't just be a tourist after reading this book. You'll be greater than a tourist!

-Alan Warner, Grand Rapids, USA

Even though I only have three days to spend in San Miguel in an upcoming visit, I will use the author's suggestions to guide some of my time there. An easy read - with chapters named to guide me in directions I want to go.

-Robert Catapano, USA

Great insights from a local perspective! Useful information and a very good value!

-Sarah, USA

This series provides an in-depth experience through the eyes of a local. Reading these series will help you to travel the city in with confidence and it'll make your journey a unique one.

-Andrew Teoh, Ipoh, Malaysia

>TOURIST

# GREATER THAN A TOURIST- BATH SOMERSET UNITED KINGDOM

*50 Travel Tips from a Local*

Sami Cheung

Greater Than a Tourist- Bath Somerset United Kingdom Copyright © 2022 by CZYK Publishing LLC. All Rights Reserved.
This book contains some information about alcohol.
All rights reserved. No part of this book may be reproduced in any form or by any electronic or mechanical means including information storage and retrieval systems, without permission in writing from the author. The only exception is by a reviewer, who may quote short excerpts in a review.

The statements in this book are of the authors and may not be the views of CZYK Publishing or Greater Than a Tourist.
First Edition
Cover designed by: Ivana Stamenkovic
Cover Image: https://pixabay.com/photos/bath-bath-uk-england-uk-britain-4278522/

**CZYK**
PUBLISHING

CZYK Publishing Since 2011.
CZYKPublishing.com
Greater Than a Tourist

Mill Hall, PA
All rights reserved.
ISBN: 9798359967570

# >TOURIST
## 50 TRAVEL TIPS FROM A LOCAL

>TOURIST

# BOOK DESCRIPTION

With travel tips and culture in our guidebooks written by a local, it is never too late to visit Bath. Greater Than a Tourist – Bath Somerset United Kingdom by author Sami Cheung offers first-hand and personal insight into the best ways to visit the beautiful, historic city of Bath. Most travel books tell you how to travel like a tourist. Although there is nothing wrong with that, as part of the 'Greater Than a Tourist' series, this book will give you candid travel tips from someone who has lived at your next travel destination. This guide book will not tell you exact addresses or store hours but instead gives you knowledge that you may not find in other smaller print travel books. Experience cultural, culinary delights, and attractions with the guidance of a Local. Slow down and get to know the people with this invaluable guide. By the time you finish this book, you will be eager and prepared to discover new activities at your next travel destination.

Inside this travel guide book you will find:
 Visitor information from a Local
 Tour ideas and inspiration
 Valuable guidebook information


   Greater Than a Tourist- A Travel Guidebook with 50 Travel Tips from a Local. Slow down, stay in one place, and get to know the people and culture. By the time you finish this book, you will be eager and prepared to travel to your next destination.

\>TOURIST

# OUR STORY

Traveling is a passion of the Greater than a Tourist book series creator. Lisa studied abroad in college, and for their honeymoon Lisa and her husband toured Europe. During her travels to Malta, an older man tried to give her some advice based on his own experience living on the island since he was a young boy. She was not sure if she should talk to the stranger but was interested in his advice. When traveling to some places she was wary to talk to locals because she was afraid that they weren't being genuine. Through her travels, Lisa learned how much locals had to share with tourists. Lisa created the Greater Than a Tourist book series to help connect people with locals. A topic that locals are very passionate about sharing.

>TOURIST

# TABLE OF CONTENTS

Book Description
Our Story
Table of Contents
Dedication
About the Author
How to Use This Book
From the Publisher
WELCOME TO > TOURIST

---
An Introduction to Bath
---

1. Welcome to Bath!
2. What's So Special About Bath?
3. History of Bath
4. Pictures to Take

Eating & Drinking in Bath

5. Great Spots for Breakfast & Brunch
6. Visit a Farm Shop (or Two!)
7. The Quintessentially English Afternoon Tea
8. The Great Sally Lunn vs Bath Bun Debate
9. The Not-So-Secret Supper Club Culture
10. Try Some Local Cuisine
11. Best Places for a Night Out
12. Unusual Spots for Eateries
13. Bath's Street Food Scene

14. Sweet Cravings
15. Delicious Drinks
16. Don't Drink the Water!

## Things to Do in Bath

17. Bath Christmas Market
18. Visit in July for Bath Carnival
19. A Mecca for Jane Austen Fans
20. More Festivals Worth a Mention
21. Bath Music Scene
22. Bath Art Scene
23. Places to Walk
24. Royal Victoria Park
25. Other Great Parks
26. Can't Miss Attractions for Kids
27. The Best Places to Shop
28. Bath is a Rugby Town
29. Unusual Ways of Seeing Bath
30. Off the Beaten Path – Cool Places to Visit Outside of Bath

>TOURIST

## Useful Things to Know

31. How to Get Around
32. Accessibility
33. Where to Stay
34. Where to Buy Some Groceries
35. Best times to Visit
36. Currency to Carry
37. You Won't Need a Dictionary!
38. Dress for the Weather
39. These Boots are Made for Walking
40. Where to Go for a Helping Hand
41. Don't Forget These Essentials!
42. Travel Safely
43. LGBTQ+ Travellers
44. Public Holidays
45. Easy to Work Out Sales Tax AKA VAT
46. Clean and Functioning Public Toilets
47. Parking & EV Charge Points
48. Social Media to Follow
49. Some Hot Tips for Souvenirs to Bring Home

## The Final Word

50. Slow Down!
TOP REASONS TO BOOK THIS TRIP
List of Photo Sources
Packing and Planning Tips
Travel Questions
Travel Bucket List
NOTES

# DEDICATION

This book is dedicated to Richie, who has always encouraged me to follow my dreams and to be more than I ever believed possible. Without you, I wouldn't be here in Bath.

To my children, Emily and Jamie, who are my everything and my inspiration. We brought you to Bath to live a happier and freer life. I love how that's turning out.

A special thank you goes to Emily, Maya, Josie and Chiho, AKA Brownie Group 487, who have helped me write some of the wonderful tips you'll read in this book. And of course, thank you to Melanie, who leads the Brownies with extreme patience and creativity!

## ABOUT THE AUTHOR

Sami is a mother, wife and dreamer, who loves to write and travel. She has lived in Bath for nine years after making the decision to raise her family there. A self-confessed workaholic, she left the financial services to pursue her creative voice and today finds herself a writer, voiceover artist and amateur jeweller. Her love of travel has brought her to far flung places like Japan, Argentina, and the USA, but somehow she always finds her way home, again.

Contact the author at:
greaterthanatouristbath@gmail.com

>TOURIST

# HOW TO USE THIS BOOK

The *Greater Than a Tourist* book series was written by someone who has lived in an area for over three months. The goal of this book is to help travelers either dream or experience different locations by providing opinions from a local. The author has made suggestions based on their own experiences. Please check before traveling to the area in case the suggested places are unavailable.

**Travel Advisories**: As a first step in planning any trip abroad, check the Travel Advisories for your intended destination.

https://travel.state.gov/content/travel/en/traveladvisories/traveladvisories.html

>TOURIST

# FROM THE PUBLISHER

Traveling can be one of the most important parts of a person's life. The anticipation and memories that you have are some of the best. As a publisher of the Greater Than a Tourist, as well as the popular *50 Things to Know* book series, we strive to help you learn about new places, spark your imagination, and inspire you. Wherever you are and whatever you do I wish you safe, fun, and inspiring travel.

Lisa Rusczyk Ed. D.
CZYK Publishing

>TOURIST

# WELCOME TO
# > TOURIST

>TOURIST

Bath is famous world-wide for its stunning architecture and Roman links. But it's so much more than just its buildings. Having moved from the Big Smoke of London to Bath, I learnt to appreciate the tranquillity, peacefulness and simple beauty of this historic city. Slowing down my pace through life was the best thing that could have happened to me, and I hope that your travels here will be equally relaxing.

*Photo 1: View of Kelston Round Hill in January*

>TOURIST

# AN INTRODUCTION TO BATH

*"I really believe I shall always be talking of Bath, when I am at home again–I do like it so very much…. Oh! Who can ever be tired of Bath"*

*-Jane Austen, Northanger Abbey*

Bath
UK

>TOURIST

# Bath Somerset UK Climate

|  | High | Low |
|---|---|---|
| January | 45 | 35 |
| February | 46 | 35 |
| March | 51 | 38 |
| April | 56 | 40 |
| May | 62 | 46 |
| June | 67 | 51 |
| July | 71 | 55 |
| August | 70 | 55 |
| September | 65 | 51 |
| October | 58 | 46 |
| November | 51 | 40 |
| December | 47 | 36 |

## GreaterThanaTourist.com

Temperatures are in Fahrenheit degrees.
Source: NOAA

>TOURIST

# 1. WELCOME TO BATH!

Everyone always says how friendly and welcoming their hometown is. Well, Bath is no exception. As a former Londoner, the first thing that struck me upon making Bath my permanent base was just how friendly people were. I'd lived in the centre of London for over a decade and could count on one hand the number of times I'd spoken to my neighbours. Not so in Bath! Wherever I go, people on their morning dog walks will offer me a "Good Morning", runners down by the River Avon will shout a breathless "Hello!" and oftentimes while walking through the city centre, I will spot a familiar face.

So, when you make your way to our little corner of the world, be sure to say "Good Morning" or "Hello", if it takes your fancy. You'll be surprised how many replies, smiles and nods you'll get in return.

And if it's your first time in Bath (and even if it's not), if you need some help, keep an eye out for the Bath BID Ambassadors. This wonderful bunch of volunteers dedicate their free time to offering a friendly face and a welcome to anyone and everyone who comes to Bath. They can offer you advice, recommendations and even directions! They're easy to spot – just keep an eye out for the bright blue "Welcome to Bath" jackets.

# 2. WHAT'S SO SPECIAL ABOUT BATH?

*"There are loads of buskers. My favourite buskers are Michael, the guitar player, and Nik, the violin player."*

-Josie, Bathonian, Age 9

Setting foot into Bath is like being transported back in time. Not only is Bath home to the Roman Baths, one of the best preserved and well-known spas of ancient times, but the beautiful Georgian architecture has been lovingly maintained, helping Bath to retain its culture and character. Bath is so well looked after that it was awarded UNESCO World Heritage Site status in 1987 – the only whole city in the UK to receive this title.

>TOURIST

*Photo 2: The Great Bath, Roman Baths*

With so many breathtaking sites and monuments, from the world-famous Royal Crescent to pretty Pulteney Bridge, it may be easy to spend your entire visit simply meandering around and admiring the sights. But don't forget that Bath is also home to countless theatres and museums, including the Theatre Royal, Holburne Museum and even the Bath Postal Museum.

When you've whetted your cultural appetite, then head down to the city centre for a little shopping. Bath is world-class at bringing together the old and the new, cleverly blending the modern high street shops of Southgate with the quaint independents around Milsom St and Walcott St. The myriad of passages and streets will have you wandering around for the best part of an afternoon, leaving you ready for a spot of afternoon tea or dinner at any one of the delectable restaurants on offer.

With its natural thermal springs, Bath lives up to its reputation as the city of wellbeing and you can't visit, without a trip to one of the many relaxing spas. The most well-known is the Thermae Bath Spa, where you'll be able to spend the day discovering the benefits of Bath's hot springs for yourself.

Bath is a great place for families to spend time together. The vast number of parks and green spaces provide ample opportunity for safe, fun play for younger children, while older families will enjoy taking lovely country walks dotted in and around the city.

There really is something for everyone in Bath. From arts and culture through to shopping and dining, you'll find it hard to be bored in Bath!

\>TOURIST

# 3. HISTORY OF BATH

Bath is a city steeped in history. You only need to take a quick stroll through the city centre to appreciate the little moments of time that have been preserved for all to see.

If you take a walk down Stall Street and Union Street, you'll find the Thermae Bath Spa on one side, which carefully houses Bath's ancient geothermal hot springs in an ultramodern building known as the "Glass Cube" and the historic Georgian Hot and Cross Baths building. A little further along, on the other side of the road, you'll find the ancient ruins of Aquae Sulis inside a classic Georgian building, now known as the Roman Baths. Continuing in this direction, you'll eventually reach the Assembly Rooms, another beautiful example of classic Georgian architecture.

This is just a little glimpse of the rich history that awaits you when you visit Bath. So if your interest has well and truly been piqued, then what are you waiting for?! Get online and book a visit here, quick!

# 4. PICTURES TO TAKE

*"Royal Crescent, Bath Abbey and Beckford's Tower are some amazing places to take pictures."*

-Chiho, Bathonian, Age 9

*Photo 3: Bath Abbey*

Everyone takes photos of places that they've been to on their travels. For some people, it's just the done thing. For others, it's a valuable memory prompt for a

>TOURIST

precious moment in time. There's little doubt that Bath is full of places to take lots of pretty pictures, and you'll need to make sure you've got a spare memory card for your camera!

Spots that are popular with tourists include all of the main attractions – the Royal Crescent, Bath Abbey, and Roman Baths to name a few. These landmarks are amazing, both to look at and if you appreciate the skill that went into constructing them long ago. Of course, the popularity of these attractions means that if you want a really good photo, you'll need to go early in the morning or late at night, when there are fewer people around.

My personal favourite spots for photos tend to be a little more off the beaten path. Walking through the Two Tunnels Greenway, a disused railway tunnel turned cycle path, you emerge near the village of Monkton Combe. Here you'll find the secluded and very picturesque Tucking Mill Reservoir. Full of wildlife and often used by anglers, it's a lovely spot for pictures.

For some great shots of Bath as a whole, you need to head up high. A few good spots include Alexandra Park, Bath City Farm, and Beckford's Tower. I often like to take a walk along the Kennet and Avon Canal, heading in the direction of Bathampton (where you'll find a couple of lovely English pubs for your efforts!). Along the way, you'll take a walk past the newly renovated Cleveland Pool and if you take a look behind you, you may be able to spot the Bath Abbey in the distance. Point and shoot!

>TOURIST

# EATING & DRINKING IN BATH

# 5. GREAT SPOTS FOR BREAKFAST & BRUNCH

With its scenic architecture and quirky side streets, Bath is a popular place for breakfast and brunch, for both tourists and locals alike. Wander around the city centre on a sunny Sunday afternoon and you're bound to see plenty of people enjoying an al-fresco brunch. Popular places include Boston Tea Party (get there early on weekends!), the Wild Cafe, and Café Retro. Most breakfast and brunch places offer the usual fare of a traditional Full English – a hearty meal that consists of bacon, sausages, your choice of eggs, baked bean, fried tomatoes or mushrooms (or both), black pudding and a side of toast. It's not for the faint-hearted!

Increasingly, veggie and vegan visitors need not worry about finding great food options, as many restaurants have some delicious plant-based alternatives. For a dedicated plant-based eatery, head over to Rooted Café on Chelsea Road for a really hearty and tasty breakfast.

If you fancy your brunch with a view, then take a drive over to the Hare & Hounds pub. A wonderful pub at any time of day, it's perfect for sampling local brews, but brunch here is truly delicious. It doesn't hurt that you're treated to a gorgeous view over the rolling Bath countryside.

*Photo 4: Enjoying the View from the Hare and Hound over Brunch*

# 6. VISIT A FARM SHOP (OR TWO!)

As Bath is located in the heart of the Somerset countryside, it should come as no surprise that there are lots of farms here! Like many parts of the world, farming and agriculture has been on the decline for many years. But more enterprising farmers have started to diversify and use their high-quality, fresh local produce to attract visitors. Here are a few of my favourite farm shop destinations.

>TOURIST

Just outside Bath, in the little village of Newton St Loe, you'll find Newton Farm Shop and Café, where you can enjoy fresh, homemade meals that mostly feature produce that has been grown and reared on the farm. It's open for breakfast and lunch, seven days per week. After your meal (if you can even bear to look at more food!), browse the farm shop for some wonderful local produce.

A little further afield, you'll find Farrington's in the village of Farrington Gurney. As well as a farm shop and café, Farrington's has revamped itself as a family-friendly destination. You'll be hard-pressed to persuade young children to leave the Playbarn – a brightly coloured indoor soft play that will entertain your children for hours. There's also an outdoor adventure park and you'll be able to visit some of the farm animals, enjoy a tractor ride or pick a Halloween pumpkin!

Bath has a few working farms within the main city, which are great places to pass the time, whether you've got kids or not. Bath City Farm is a much-loved Bath charity in Twerton, which is dedicated to bringing together a community through nature and farming. It runs a wide range of groups and classes for toddlers, teens and adults, all aimed at improving mental health and wellbeing. Its farm café opened in 2022 and is a terrific venue for sampling food that's been grown on the farm, as well as enjoying rolling views across Bath.

# 7. THE QUINTESSENTIALLY ENGLISH AFTERNOON TEA

You simply cannot visit Bath without indulging in afternoon tea. The practice of enjoying finger sandwiches, cakes and tea was made fashionable by the seventh Duchess of Bedford, Anna, around 1840 AD.

Back in its heyday, afternoon tea was an important social event and women would wear their best dresses for the occasion. Today, afternoon tea is still a social event and getting dressed up for it is part of the fun!

For a spectacular afternoon tea, book yourself into the Bath Pump Room. Built above the Roman Baths in 1704, then remodelled in 1751 and rebuilt in 1796, the Bath Pump Room is an elegant setting that was favoured by the upper classes whenever they visited Bath. Today it's a lovely restaurant and serves afternoon tea daily, accompanied by live musicians. If you're able to visit Bath at Christmas time, then be sure to book your afternoon tea table – I promise you, there's no experience quite like it.

Other great places for afternoon tea include the Royal Crescent Hotel and the Bath Priory. The selection of patisseries at the Royal Crescent Hotel includes their take on the traditional Bath Bun, which is well worth the visit (This is hands down my favourite Bath Bun!). You may even bump into a

>TOURIST

celebrity or two! If you're visiting Bath in the summer months, ask to have your afternoon tea on the terrace and enjoy the beautifully landscaped gardens at both hotels.

There are so many places in Bath that offer afternoon tea that you may find it hard to choose just one! Of course, you could always come back for another visit…

# 8. THE GREAT SALLY LUNN VS BATH BUN DEBATE

Two of Bath's best known sweet treats are the Sally Lunn Bunn and the Bath Bun. Even Jane Austen was known to have enjoyed a Bath bunn and once wrote a letter explaining how she had been "disordering my stomach with Bath bunns". To this day, there is a huge debate over which of these two buns is the superior bun.

A Sally Lunn Bunn is a plain, round bun that looks like a bap or roll, but tastes more like French brioche – light, sweet and buttery. Made to a secret receipt, it's usually enjoyed freshly warmed and smeared in cinnamon butter. You can get yours from Sally Lunn's, one of the oldest restaurants in Bath. The building also features a kitchen museum in Bath, which will delight any little ones you may have in tow.

The Bath Bun is a smaller, stickier bun than the Sally Lunn Bunn and can be purchased from the Bath Bun Tea Shoppe. This sweet bun is topped with delightful crystals of sugar and sweet raisins. The bun was originally created by Dr William Oliver, who was born in Cornwall in 1695, for his patients. These delightful delicates are light and sweet, and often have a little clump of sugar crystals in the centre.

Why not grab both and join the great debate?

# 9. THE NOT-SO-SECRET SUPPER CLUB CULTURE

Foodie culture has really exploded in Bath in the last few years. The annual Great Bath Feast is usually held in September and showcases some of the best food and drink in the South West. While restaurants, cafés and bars are still popular throughout the city, it's supper club culture that has really taken off.

A supper club, also known as a pop-up restaurant, operates from a temporary venue and sometimes, even someone's home. They're great ways to sample new cuisines and meet new people and the supper club movement in Bath is simply booming!

One of the most popular supper clubs in Bath is held at Noya's Kitchen every Friday. Guests are

>TOURIST

served a five-course meal, all hand chosen and cooked by Noya, herself. It's a cosy, intimate experience, and features some delicious Vietnamese cuisine. Like many supper clubs, you won't be able to just walk in on your chosen night, so if you have your heart set on visiting Noya's Supper Club then book ahead as waiting lists are in operation (I've been known to wait six months for a table!). Alternatively, Noya's Kitchen is also open for lunch, Tuesday - Saturday, which may be a more practical way of sampling some authentic Vietnamese food, if you're pressed for time.

Over at Castle Farm in Midford, their weekly Saturday supper club serves a five- or six-course menu, based on a monthly theme. Previous themes have included a Studio Ghibli night, an Indian Feast, and a Tarantino-inspired menu. Always themed to perfection, the Castle Farm supper club is an experience to remember.

Bath is also home to Ping's Makan Club, which is the brainchild of 2014 MasterChef Champion, Ping Coombes. The Makan Club runs monthly at different venues around Bath, and serves delicious Malaysian-inspired dishes all created by none other than Ping, herself. Ping has the wonderful ability to make people feel at ease, so you're guaranteed to leave the supper club with a few more friends, as well as a full stomach!

# 10. TRY SOME LOCAL CUISINE

When I think of English cuisine, I can think of a few traditional foods – fish and chips, a Sunday roast, and pub grub. I may be biased, but Bath has plenty of all three!

Fish and chips is a Friday night British staple. In my humble opinion, a good fish and chips should have light, crispy batter, sweet and fresh fish, and fluffy, crispy chips. The Scallop Shell is the winner of the 2019 National Fish and Chip Awards and for good reason! You'll only be able to dine-in here, but it's worth it and there's a wide range of seafood options if you don't quite fancy the heaviness of a traditional fish and chips. Other great fish and chip options include the Oyster Shell, Pollocks and Sea Pearl.

A Sunday roast is the traditional Sunday lunch in the UK. A roasted meat – chicken, beef, pork and lamb are all common – is served alongside vegetables, roast potatoes, Yorkshire puddings and lashings of gravy. The Marlborough Tavern and Hare and Hounds are great options for a hearty Sunday roast.

On the topic of pub grub more generally, the quality of pub food has risen quite dramatically over recent years. There's a whole food trend for gastropubs. Gone are the days of soggy pasta and lukewarm steaks. The Locksbrook Inn and Bathampton Mill are great options for some great pub grub. Of course, a good English pub should also have a lovely beer garden and the Boathouse, Hop Pole and Hare and Hounds won't disappoint on that front.

# 11. BEST PLACES FOR A NIGHT OUT

With two universities in Bath, it's unsurprising that the nightlife is buzzing. University students are often found in the city's various nightclubs, which include Labyrinth, Zero/Zero, Second Bridge and the great Bath institution, Moles, which has been entertaining students and locals alike, since 1978.

If nightclubs aren't quite your cup of tea, then Bath also offers some sophisticated bars. Try Dos Dedos on Bartlett Street, a quirky Mexican cantina serving up authentic tequilas and tacos. For great drinks and laughs, head over to Komedia. This brilliant community-owned entertainment venue is host to over 400 different live events per year and showcases some of the best comedy, music and cabaret acts in the UK.

But for something truly unique, visit the Sleight Bar in the city centre. Here you'll be able to enjoy great drinks, great company and some great close-up magic! Since it's Bath's only magic bar, there really isn't any experience quite like it in the city.

# 12. UNUSUAL SPOTS FOR EATERIES

Bath's proud World Heritage status can be a bit of a double-edged sword. While it brings in a vital economic boost by attracting visitors from all over the world, it also means that it's quite tricky to obtain planning permission to change the façade of any of the buildings. So, Bathonians have gotten creative in making the best use of every inch of the city's space and you'll find restaurants and cafés in some pretty unusual places.

Along the North Parade, you'll find several restaurants located in the vaults of the historic terrace building located there. Many of these vaults were originally built for storage, as well as to support the roads and buildings above them. But today, at restaurants like Sotto Sotto, La Perla and Opa Bath, you'll not only enjoy a delicious meal but you'll also be able to get a glimpse of the mysterious subterranean world of Bath. A word of warning, these restaurants can be quite small and cosy, so you're best advised to book ahead.

Over near the Bath Spa Railway Station, you'll find that many of the Grade I* Listed railway arches have been remodelled as restaurants and eateries. This development was opened in phases dating back to 2009, and the railway arches are now home to a number of restaurant chains.

# 13. BATH'S STREET FOOD SCENE

Street food is a growing trend across the UK, and Bath is no exception. Festivals and events tend to draw in huge numbers of street food vendors at certain times of the year. If you love street food, keep an eye out for the Big Bath Feast and the Bath Christmas Market, where you'll be able to enjoy some great street food and a fun-filled atmosphere.

A few street food vendors are based in Bath year-round. Just around the corner from the Roman Baths, the Hot Sausage Company cart is a familiar sight (and smell!) for locals. Stop by for a quick hot dog on your way to queue for the Roman Baths. Over in Southgate, you'll find LJ Hugs serving mouthwatering Cajun food – I challenge you to walk past this stand without stopping to order!

If you're looking for a little cover, then head over to Green Park Station, which is home to the likes of the Thai Hut, Maureen's Mediterranean Street Food, and the Honey Hut. There's plenty of seating and it's all sheltered from the wind and rain. On the weekends, you'll find the Green Park Station Saturday Market or the Bath Farmers Market, where you'll be able to enjoy more local Somerset produce.

# 14. SWEET CRAVINGS

By now you've read about Sally Lunn Bunns, Bath Buns and afternoon tea. So you know that there are plenty of sweet treats to be found in Bath. But in my opinion, no holiday is complete without an ice cream (or three!)

Bath is home to Marshfield Farm Real Dairy Ice Cream, a multi award-winning ice cream. Rich and creamy, the ice cream is made from milk that is sourced directly from the farm, so it's about as local as you can get. Many shops and cafés in the city centre stock this delicious sweet treat, but if you're around in the summer months, head over to Marshfield Farm's ice cream parlour where you can enjoy your ice cream (almost) straight from the cow.

In the city centre, you're treated to a huge variety of ice cream shops. No two Bath ice cream shops are the same, so an ice cream shop crawl may be the only way to fairly decide on your favourite! But if you're in a hurry, here are a few of my favourites.

Swoon Gelato is perfect for smooth, creamy gelato style ice cream, or a full-sized gelato cake if you're celebrating a special occasion. Be warned though – they only have a small number of tables, so expect to get a takeaway and for the queues to be long in the summer-time! At Creams Café, you can enjoy American-style ice creams and desserts – the portions are huge, so you may want to share if you still want to leave room for dinner! If you've just finished wandering around the Roman Baths, then David Thayer's ice cream shop is just around the corner, or a little further up, you can grab a cone at the Real Italian Ice Cream Co for some more unusual flavours (green apple ice cream, anyone?).

Suffice to say, you're not short of ice cream choices here in Bath!

# 15. DELICIOUS DRINKS

If you're looking to sample a local tipple, then you're in luck as Bath is home to a couple of locally brewed beverages.

For a robust, full-bodied beer, grab a bottle or glass of Bath Gem. It's Bath Ales' flagship amber ale and was their first brewed beer. Head over to the Hop Pole where you can grab a glass and head out to their hidden beer garden to relax.

If you're more of a spirit drinker, then head to the Bath Distillery Gin Bar, where you can sample locally distilled gin. Better yet, check out the whole range of Bath Gins via the bar's "Gin Austen" menu – a fun and elegant way to sample some creative cocktails, with a little nod to the great writer.

# 16. DON'T DRINK THE WATER!

So I'm not talking about regular tap water. That's totally fine to drink, straight from the tap. Do note that Bath is a hard water area and so you may wish to filter your water before you drink it.

What I'm actually talking about is the spa water that you can taste at the Roman Baths. Yes, I know the whole reason Bath came into being was the therapeutic properties of the hot spring water, bubbling beneath the earth's surfaces. But hear me out.

When you visit the Roman Baths, you have the option of trying a glass of Bath's famous spa water. It contains around 43 different minerals and has been drunk for thousands of years for its perceived healing properties. While it's perfectly fine to drink, I think it's a bit of an acquired taste. I'm only thankful that you no longer have to pay for the privilege. If you're looking for the full, authentic Bath experience, then the Roman Baths spa water is a must-try – just don't say I didn't warn you!

>TOURIST

# THINGS TO DO IN BATH

# 17. BATH CHRISTMAS MARKET

Many UK cities host an annual Christmas market and Bath is no exception to the rule. Each November, around 150 pop-up chalets magically appear around the city, courtesy of Santa's elves (AKA our friendly, local council). Bath is completely transformed for a few weeks of the year for a fabulously fun, festive experience.

The Bath Christmas Market is extremely popular, so if you did drive in for your trip, I highly recommend leaving the car in its designated parking spot and walking or bussing into the town centre. Grab yourself a cup of mulled wine or hot chocolate and leisurely meander your way through the cobbled streets of Bath, taking in the festive sights and smells. The Christmas Market is spread across the whole of the city centre and it gets very crowded, so don't expect to get anywhere in a hurry!

I personally find myself heading straight to the chalet selling Rubis chocolate wine, and make sure I stock up on a bottle every year. If you've never had chocolate wine before, I'd recommend you stop by for a complimentary sample. I know I do!

At the Bath Christmas Market, you'll find plenty of handcrafted goodies sourced from across the South

West and lots and lots of delicious, traditional festive treats like hot roasted chestnuts and German bratwurst! All around the Market, you'll be treated to live performances, fake snow and the beautiful Bath Christmas lights.

It's the perfect opportunity to get into the festive spirit as well as to stock up on Christmas presents and decorations.

## 18. VISIT IN JULY FOR BATH CARNIVAL

For some free entertainment (yes, I said FREE!), join us in July for the annual Bath Carnival. Each year, a huge party atmosphere colourfully explodes onto the streets of Bath, celebrating carnival arts in all its glory. The creativity of local talented artists is on full display, with bright, intricate carnival costumes, amazing dance choreography and spine-tingling musical compositions.

The carnival procession winds its way along its city centre route, while historic Sydney Gardens is host to live bands, DJs, and lots of creative workshops and kid-friendly activities. Bath is always packed out for this event, so it's another one to head to on foot or public transport.

>TOURIST

# 19. A MECCA FOR JANE AUSTEN FANS

Fans of Jane Austen need to make the pilgrimage to Bath. Between 1801-1806, Jane Austen called Bath her home and even used the city as the backdrop to two out of her six published books – "Northanger Abbey" and "Persuasion". The city has also been used as a film location for many TV and film adaptations of Austen's books, including the latest Netflix film version of "Persuasion".

If you're a fan of Austen's literary works or even if you're just curious about what all the fuss is about, then head over to the Jane Austen Centre on Gay Street. There's usually a gent dressed in Regency Costume at the door to greet you, and you literally feel like you're stepping back in time. The Jane Austen Centre is *the* place to go for all things Jane and regularly organise walking tours and talks. The Regency tea room is kitted out in period decoration and serves cream teas on a daily basis.

And if that's not enough Jane Austen for you, then plan your visit for the month of September. For 10 whole days, Bath hosts the Jane Austen Festival – the world's largest and longest running Jane Austen Festival in the whole world! Running for over 20 years, it even holds the Guiness World Record for the "Largest Gathering of People Dressed in Regency

Costumes". (The record was 409 people and hasn't been broken since 2009!)

The festival kicks off with a Regency Costumed Parade, which draws plenty of spectators. During the festival, you can enjoy a huge number of Jane Austen inspired events, from guided walks, theatrical performances and workshops. The festivities culminate in the annual Jane Austen Festival Ball, an event not to be missed by Austen fans.

# 20. MORE FESTIVALS WORTH A MENTION

Bath is a gold mine for cultural activities and its festival calendar is usually jam-packed. There are probably far too many festivals to mention, but here are a few of my favourites.

Kicking off with the Great Bath Feast because who doesn't love to eat yummy food? Usually taking place in September, this is the perfect place to sample the best of the South West's thriving culinary scene. You'll have the chance to see some great demos, learn tips from some of the best chefs and of course, devour lots of tasty dishes.

The Bath Festival takes place in the spring-time, and is a celebration of music and books. The Bath Children's Literature Festival takes place in the autumn and is a two week programme full of talks and activities, which aim to inspire a love of reading in children. Both festivals are quite magical and there are lots of fun things to do, like making puppets inspired by Alice in Wonderland, watching an interactive play or meeting a favourite book character.

With such beautiful surroundings, Bath would be remiss if it didn't celebrate its landscape. The Bathscape Walking Festival takes place in the autumn, when the heat of the summer has broken but the frequent rains of the latter part of the year haven't quite reached us yet (fingers crossed!). All of the events are centred around walking, which gives you a fantastic opportunity to see Bath on foot. There are also plenty of themed talks and events, such as bat walks, learning about trees or exploring the LGBTQ+ history of Bath.

In September, many of Bath's best known sites and buildings fling open their doors to the public as part of the Heritage Open Days, the UK's largest community heritage festival. The best part of it is that it's all completely free! Sites that have taken part in the past include the newly restored Cleveland Pools, the UK's oldest lido, Prior Park Landscape Garden, and Dyrham Park, a 17th century baroque mansion.

# 21. BATH MUSIC SCENE

Put Bath and music together in the same sentence and you'll probably conjure up images of choirs singing at the Bath Abbey. While those are highly recommended and feature lots of local, talented individuals, the Bath music scene is much, much broader.

Popular music venues include the Forum and Komedia. Both regularly have a selection of mainstream and lesser-known artists, so there's always something for everyone. Local pubs and venues will also regularly have live music performances, so stopping by the pub for a pint might lead you to discovering a new favourite talent.

In the summer, Pub in the Park is hosted in Royal Victoria Park and is a fantastic day out for trying foods by some of the best local chefs, as well as enjoying a lively outdoor concert. If you happen to be in Bath in May, then you'll be treated to some excellent local music performances courtesy of the Bath Festival programme.

>TOURIST

# 22. BATH ART SCENE

Bath is a thriving cultural and art centre and is home to several different art galleries and museums.

The Victoria Art Gallery is in the city centre, next to the stunning Pulteney Weir, and hosts a collection of permanent art works spanning the 15th century to present day. The ground floor features two ever-changing temporary exhibition spaces, so you'll always find something new, even if you're a regular visitor to Bath. The folks at Victoria Art Gallery are also experts at putting on fun activities for younger art lovers.

The Holburne Museum is located at the edge of Sydney Gardens. It also features a number of permanent art galleries with lots of interesting artefacts on display, the bulk of which were collected by Sir Thomas William Holburne. Feature exhibitions of contemporary and classic artists help to keep the museum fresh and the last Friday of each month is dedicated to "Up Late Friday", where you can visit the museum after opening hours, free of charge.

The local art scene is also thriving. Events like the Newbridge Art Trail give you a small insight into Bath's art world, when local artists open their studios to the general public. The event usually takes place in September and you'll be able to see artists at work, as well as take part in various workshops and events.

# 23. PLACES TO WALK

*"Kelston Round Hill has beautiful scenery and awesome views. Take a football and enjoy!"*

-Maya, Bathonian, Age 9

*Photo 5: Taking an autumn walk along the Cotswold Way*

Located in the valley of the River Avon, Bath boasts some wonderful walks. Some walks are more challenging than others due to the hilly surroundings, but it's well worth the effort for the scenic views.

Head up to Kelston Round Hill for some spectacular views of Bath. On a clear day, you can

>TOURIST

even see out to Wales and catch glimpses of the Severn Bridge (old and new). Join the path at Deanhill Lane or Broadmoor Lane. The route is circular, so you won't need to worry about losing your way back to the car, if you've brought one. While the route involves some hills, they're quite manageable even with children in tow. If you have time, then head out towards Kelston village where you'll find the Bath Soft Cheese Café and some amazing food.

From Weston Village, you can also take a walk up to Beckford's Tower. It takes around 40-45 minutes at a brisk pace. Here you'll not only be able to take in the amazing panoramic views, but also learn about William Beckford, his accomplishments in architecture and the realities of his links to the slave trade.

On the east side of Bath, you'll find the village of Batheaston, which is another great starting point for some beautiful walks. Here you can find your way to Little Solsbury Hill, which was the inspiration for Peter Gabriel's song, "Solsbury Hill".

There are so many beautiful places to visit, both in the city centre and on the outskirts, so grab your walking shoes and take a walk around Bath. You won't regret it.

# 24. ROYAL VICTORIA PARK

Bath is blessed with several parks throughout the city, perfect for relaxing and slowing down a notch.

The most well-known of Bath's parks is Royal Victoria Park. Fondly known by locals as "Vicky Park", it was opened in 1830 AD by an 11-year-old Princess Victoria (who grew up to become Queen Victoria). Vicky Park is a huge 57-acre green space that will appeal to both kids and grown-ups. In fact, it's so large that it warranted a whole tip all to itself.

The park is home to a very popular children's play area, complete with a coffee shop, merry-go-round and skate park. If your kids particularly like merry-go-rounds or bouncy castles, make sure you've got some change as these have a small charge to play. The rest of the park is free. Across the road from the kids' playground, you'll find a divine duck pond, where you can while away some time feeding the wildlife (do watch out for the seagulls, though!).

Heading up the hill from the play area, you'll find Bath's Botanical Gardens, which is a lovely landscaped garden area and often used as a wedding venue. In the summer months, you can join the free Park Yoga classes, for some relaxing stretching.

At the very top of the park, the Great Dell is the perfect space for little adventurers. This secluded

>TOURIST

woodland is a magical place, with lots of logs to climb and secret dens to explore. When it's time for a rest, set your little ones the challenge of finding the Star Wars bench.

*Photo 6: In the Great Dell, Royal Victoria Park*

The main part of the park is perfect for picnics and BBQs (you can only use disposable BBQ grills in the designated areas) and is often used to host events and temporary attractions. From time-to-time, you'll find a pop-up funfair or large-scale event like Pub in the Park. I often take a wander over and watch everyone hard at work making the area safe for the next event.

If you're looking to bring a little greenery home, head over to the Urban Garden Centre, which is a social enterprise that helps local people through sales of plants for the garden and home, as well as running well-being classes for the community. There's a great little café hidden inside, so pull up a chair and enjoy your surroundings.

When you've had your cuppa, head across the road to the Royal Crescent Lower Lawn. Here you'll be treated to unforgettable views of the world-famous Royal Crescent (AKA the "big banana", as dubbed by my 5-year-old son!). Have your camera ready! In the summer, the Lawn is used to host various events like outdoor cinema and some great live music acts, like Michael Bublé.

This section of the park is also home to some tennis courts and an 18-hole Adventure Golf course. In the summer, the bowls lawn is transformed into Bath on the Beach, a fun urban beach area where you can enjoy tasty cocktails, wood-fired pizzas, and great company. In the winter, the whole space is transformed again into Bath on Ice, the city's outdoor ice rink. The perfect place to enjoy some skating and cosy drinks in the run-up to Christmas.

Royal Victoria Park really does have something for everyone, and locals and tourists alike will love the space.

>TOURIST

# 25. OTHER GREAT PARKS

It would be remiss of us not to at least mention some of the other park spaces in and around Bath. Each has its own personality and many will appeal to both adults and kids. Whether you're looking for a place for a quiet walk, somewhere for a picnic or a play area, there's something for everyone.

On the eastern side of Bath, you'll find Alice Park. Although it's considerably smaller than Royal Victoria Park at 8-acres, it remains a wonderful community space designed with the whole family in mind. Here you'll find a lovely playpark, skate park and community garden, as well as (you guessed it!) a café.

In the city centre, Parade Gardens is a Grade II listed park and is open year-round. Wandering through Parade Gardens is like hopping back in time, with its quaint bandstand and perfectly manicured gardens. Take note that there is a small entrance charge to the general public to help maintain the grounds. Parade Gardens is often used as a film location, so you may have some fun trying to spot it in some of your favourite movies and TV shows.

High on a hillside to the south side of Bath is Alexandra Park, a wonderful green space that boasts panoramic views of the city. It's another perfect space for a walk or picnic, and has great connections for local walking routes.

The newly refurbished children's park in Sydney Gardens is a welcome addition to the city. The new facilities include a water play feature, basketball hoops and a climbing frame inspired by Sham Castle, as well as the usual swings and slides. Originally created as Georgian pleasure gardens, the park retains much of its original charm and is a great place for train spotters!

There are many, many more parks in and around Bath. This just gives you a little flavour of some of the places you can go to get away from the hustle and bustle of city life.

>TOURIST

# 26. CAN'T MISS ATTRACTIONS FOR KIDS

*"Playing in Victoria Park, hanging out in Thirsty Meeples, and watching the hot air balloons go up are my favourite things to do in Bath."*

*-Emily, Bathonian, Age 9*

*Photo 7: Hot air balloon leaving Royal Victoria Park*

Bath is full of amazing things for kids to do. In addition to the hugely popular parks, many of Bath's tourist attractions run kids activities. Dressing up in

Georgian outfits at the Assembly Rooms, a dedicated children's audio guide at the Roman Baths and an arts trail at the Holburne Museum, to name just a few. My kids have done all of these things, many times over!

The Egg Theatre is a dedicated children's theatre, which is attached to the Theatre Royal Bath. It's a brilliant place to introduce children and young adults to the arts, and has a full and varied programme of events. Here you can catch a show or take part in a workshop, before enjoying the family-friendly café.

For an easy, kid-friendly walk, head over to Rainbow Woods. It's a perfect spot for a picnic. Younger children will love exploring the magical fairy door trail, while older children will be able to burn off some energy in the play park.

Of course, when it's raining, you'll want to head indoors for the day and Bath has you covered there, too. At the Bath Sports and Leisure Centre, you'll find a tonne of family-friendly activities like bowling, soft play, a swimming pool and trampolining park, which will keep everyone occupied for hours. Be sure to book in advance though.

If you've got a young train enthusiast in the family, then take a trip to Bitton village, which is just outside Bath. Here you'll find the carefully preserved Avon Valley Railway. Originally opened in 1869 to provide a rail link between Birmingham and the South West, today you'll find steam trains chugging along three miles of restored track. For an extra special treat, book your visit for Christmas time when you can "wow" your little ones with a train ride and visit from Santa, himself.

A firm wet weather favourite for my family is heading over to the Thirsty Meeples café for an afternoon of hot chocolate and board games! The expert team here will be able to advise you on fun games to suit everyone in your group, and they have an unbelievable number of games (most of which I've never even heard of!) for all-ages, from 3 to 100. If you've found a new favourite game, you can even buy your own copy to take home!

# 27. THE BEST PLACES TO SHOP

Ah, shopping! Is there any better past-time when you're on holiday? I mean, after eating and sightseeing, of course.

Bath is a hot spot for independent shops and boutiques, and is such a shoppers' paradise that it draws shoppers from far and wide. You'll regularly see coaches full of visitors who've crossed the border from Wales, just to do a day's shopping. There are quite a few shopping districts in Bath, each with its own character.

The central part of Bath leading down to Southgate is packed with a mix of high street stores, independents and cafés. It tends to get busy on weekends, so plan in lots of rest stops – try some of the great independent coffee shops like Mokoko Coffee, Colonna & Small's or the Forum Coffee House. For something a little different, head over to Comins Tea where you'll be able to sample some delicious teas that have been personally sourced by owners, Michelle & Rob, as well as some of their favourite delicacies from their travels, like Japanese gyoza and Indian black rice porridge.

When your legs have sufficiently recovered or your stomach is full, hit the streets again for more shopping! Milsom Street is an oasis of boutiques and restaurants, with lots of shops stocking designer and vintage fashion as well as some quirky gift, trinket and furniture shops. Wandering along Green Street, you'll find some adorable art, photography and beauty shops as well as a butcher.

Turn left out of the bottom of Green Street, and you'll find your way over to Walcott Street, known as Bath's artisan quarter. This lovely area is full of unusual independent and vintage shops, including a very hidden away comic book store called American Dream Comics. Climb the stairs to this comic book lover's heaven, and you'll be rewarded with a wide variety of comics and graphic novels, as well as memorabilia. On Saturdays, you'll find the local flea market, full of vintage clothing and antiques.

>TOURIST

Pretty Pulteney Bridge is an unusual bridge for the UK. Spanning the River Avon, it has shops built along both sides across the length of the bridge. Its design was inspired by the Italian bridges bearing shops and reminds me of my time in Venice every time I walk across it.

If you really want to shop like a local, you need to head out of the city centre. The charming residential area of Larkhall is home to a quaint row of shops, including Larkhall Butchers, Bath's No.1 butchers, Crockadoodledoo for all your pottery craft needs, and Larkhall Deli. Across the River Avon, you'll find Moorland Roads – another Bath high street that's charmingly captured a moment in history. Here you'll find a huge range of quirky shops and restaurants, including gift shops, hardware stores, and more.

If you're a die-hard outlet shopper, you're in luck. A short drive along the M4 will find you in Swindon, where you can head to the Swindon Designer Outlet, home to a great range of discounted designer brands. Heading out in the other direction will find you in the village of Street and the infamous Clarks Village. Over 90 designer and high street brands are housed in this shopper's paradise, which is located at the site of the former Clarks' shoe factory.

## 28. BATH IS A RUGBY TOWN

Soon after moving to Bath, I learned that it's a big rugby town. Bath Rugby plays in Premiership Rugby, which is England's top division of rugby. Like most sports, rugby also has intense rivalries between clubs. Bath Rugby's main rivals are Bristol Rugby and Gloucester Rugby.

If you're hoping to take in a little British sport while you're here, then get yourself a ticket to one of Bath Rugby's fixtures. The atmosphere in the stadium and around town on match days is electric, and the city will be awash with blue, white and black striped shirts, scarves and faces!

Of course, there are lots of other sports to watch in Bath, too. The city is proudly home to Bath Cricket Club and Bath City FC.

>TOURIST

# 29. UNUSUAL WAYS OF SEEING BATH

Like many cities around the world, you can take a sightseeing bus to familiarise yourself with the city. They're a convenient way of hopping on and off, near the main attractions and sights. Bath is a very walkable city, so a walking tour can also be a great way to learn more about its history and residents. There are lots of themed walking tours, if you have a special interest, from ghost walking tours to Jane Austen and "Bridgerton" location tours.

But if you want a special way of seeing the city, then consider booking yourself onto a hot air balloon ride. They're a fantastic way of getting a birds' eye view of the city and the only way to truly appreciate the skill that underpinned the construction of many of Bath's famous landmarks, including the Royal Crescent, the Circus and the Roman Baths. Even if you intend to keep your feet firmly on the ground, watching the balloons take off from Royal Victoria Park is pretty magical.

*Photo 9: Pulteney Weir at Dusk*

Another great way of seeing some of Bath's beautiful sights is by boat. Knowledgeable tour guides will take you on a trip along the River Avon, where you can take in views of Pulteney Bridge, the Weir and Bath Abbey. Some tours even throw in a couple of glasses of Prosecco, so you can really unwind for the afternoon.

>TOURIST

# 30. OFF THE BEATEN PATH – COOL PLACES TO VISIT OUTSIDE OF BATH

Most Bath guidebooks will tell you that you must visit the neighbouring city of Bristol, which is a mere 12 miles away and around a 40-minute drive or 12 minutes by train. No doubt, it's a beautiful city, rich in culture and history and with a very different vibe from Bath. But Bristol cannot be described in a few short sentences, and it's not really off the beaten path, per se.

Nestled in the valley of the River Avon, surrounded by beautiful Royal Victoria Park and lovely stretches of river and canal, Bath is just a fantastic gateway to a vast world of quaint villages, seaside towns, and green surroundings. Here are just a few interesting places to hop over to from Bath.

First up is Chew Valley Lake, which is around a half-hour drive away from Bath. This beautiful reservoir is perfect for parking up and enjoying a leisurely walk or bike ride. The nature trails are suitable for young and old, and there's even a delightful children's play area to entertain the little ones. Best of all, the fabulous Salt & Malt fish and chip shop is located right by the side of the water, so you can enjoy a well-deserved tea-time treat after burning off some energy!

If you have a few hours spare on your itinerary, then Bradford-on-Avon is a quaint, historic town around 6 miles east of Bath. Here you can enjoy long, rambling walks along the River Avon, followed by a delicious pub lunch – a quintessentially English weekend past-time! The historic market town of Frome is also well worth a visit and lies just 15 miles outside of Bath. This charming town has a vibrant local community, boasts a wealth of independent shops and boutiques, and is home to a thriving performing arts scene. If you can time your visit for the first Sunday of the month, between the months of March to December, you'll be rewarded with the ever-changing, award-winning Frome Independent street market. Here you'll be able to stock up on lots of delicious West Country produce and handmade crafts to take home and enjoy!

If you're prepared to travel a little further afield, you'll find Bath to be a great base to visit many well-known sights, such as the world-famous Stonehenge, beautiful Glastonbury Tor, and Cheddar Gorge, home of the great English cheddar cheese. There are numerous beautiful English cities that are easily reachable from Bath, including Oxford, Birmingham, and even London. Heading towards the West could find you crossing the border to South Wales and enjoying the beautiful Welsh coast in under an hour. The options are (almost!) infinite and you'll soon find yourself wishing you had more time to explore Bath and beyond.

>TOURIST

## USEFUL THINGS TO KNOW

# 31. HOW TO GET AROUND

The first thing to strike you when you arrive in Bath is the hills! OK, perhaps that's the second thing, after the stunning architecture.

As tempting as it may be to rely on a car to get around Bath, it's not highly recommended for quite a few reasons. Bath was not really designed to accommodate cars, and one wrong turn could find you stuck down an unfamiliar, narrow road with no way to turn around (I have done it, more than once). Public parking in the city centre can also be very expensive, and it gets busy, particularly on weekends.

In recent years, the local government has really focused on environmental issues, and 2021 saw the introduction of the Clean Air Zone (CAZ to locals!). At the moment, the CAZ means that certain vehicles, like taxis, vans and some camper vans, that do not meet the required emission standards are required to pay a charge. While it doesn't yet apply to private cars and motorbikes, this could change in the future and for good reason! So check the Bath and North East Somerset Council website for the latest CAZ rules.

If you're only visiting Bath for the day, then you should consider parking up at one of the three Park &

Rides, located in Lansdown, Odd Down and Newbridge. You'll be able to park your car for free, just paying for the bus ride into the city centre.

Bath is quite a small city in the grand scheme of things, so if you're spending the day in the city centre, you'll likely find that you can comfortably walk to most places. Like most modern cities, you'll also be able to make use of the bus network, hire a bike or an e-bike, or even an electric scooter, to get around. All of these are brilliant ways to take in all of the sights of the city, at a leisurely pace.

Cycling around the city can be challenging due to its hilly nature. An e-bike can help you navigate the worst of the hills. There are plenty of cycle paths around Bath, including the Bristol and Bath Railway Path, which will take you all the way from Bath to the city of Bristol. Cycling around town can be a little trickier, as there are few dedicated cycle lanes. However, the roads are constantly being updated and the city is becoming increasingly cycle-friendly.

>TOURIST

# 32. ACCESSIBILITY

Accessibility in Bath is improving all the time. The roads increasingly have more dropped kerbs to make it easier for wheelchairs and pushchairs to cross over. Shops have started to have more ramps and wider doors to get in and out. Many shops and restaurants provide disabled toilets for customers to use.

With Bath being a World Heritage site, you'll find many of the buildings here were constructed a long time ago and are listed. It can be difficult for businesses to get the permissions needed to modify buildings to be suitable for disabled persons. There are also many roads in Bath where the pavements can get quite narrow, making them unsuitable for wheelchairs or large pushchairs. So plan ahead and be prepared to alter your route from time to time.

Awareness of disabilities has increased, so too has the efforts to ensure that attractions are as inclusive as they can be. As recently as 15 years ago, it was not possible for wheelchair users to access the Great Bath, the main pool at the Roman Baths, due to the number of stairs you had to go down. At that time, a couple of designated days were held each year to allow wheelchair access. Nowadays, accessibility has been greatly improved so that with an advanced booking, the Customer Services team will be able to assist people with their individual needs.

Bath is a very inclusive city, and makes an effort to accommodate all additional needs. Many shops have "quiet hours" for elderly people or those with hidden disabilities, such as autism. Just check the relevant websites or phone ahead to check the details.

## 33. WHERE TO STAY

On the whole, Bath is a safe and secure place to visit. There is a wide range of choices when it comes to places to stay during your visit (and constantly increasing choices, too!). From 5* hotels in the city centre, to quaint B&Bs and stylish Airbnbs, there's a place to suit everyone's tastes (and budgets).

If budget is no object, then take a look at the Royal Crescent Hotel, which is *the* choice for the rich and famous when they visit Bath (I've spotted more than one celebrity coming out when I've wandered past!). For the duration of your trip, your address will be none other than the world-famous Royal Crescent, backdrop to many movies, including 2008 film, "The Duchess", and popular Netflix drama, "Bridgerton".

>TOURIST

*Photo 8: The Royal Crescent, Bath*

For places to stay that are slightly easier on the pocket, take a look at hotel chains, smaller boutique hotels and B&Bs. If you're looking to avoid staying in the city centre, but still want easy access to the amenities, try staying in places like Widcombe, Larkhall or Newbridge. These residential areas are just far enough away from the city centre to be quiet, but close enough that you could conveniently walk or bus into town. Bath is a very walkable town in terms of distance, although your calves may suffer if they're not used to hilly terrain!

# 34. WHERE TO BUY SOME GROCERIES

If you're staying in self-catering accommodation, or just after some snacks, you may find yourself wanting to buy some groceries at some point during your trip.

Many locals frequent the larger supermarkets on the edges of the city, for better variety and convenience (you can carry all your groceries directly from the supermarket to your car in the car park). Some of the larger Bath supermarkets may require you to drive or take public transport and include Morrisons, Lidl, and the Marks & Spencer Food Hall.

If you're staying in the city centre, there's still a choice of supermarkets like Sainsbury's, Waitrose and Marks & Spencers. Some of the city centre stores tend to have longer opening hours, so you can nip out if you've run out of milk at 11pm! Just look for a Sainsbury's Local or Tesco Express.

For great quality fruit and veg at very reasonable prices, try the two lovely outdoor grocers in the town centre. Both run on Mondays, Wednesdays, Fridays and Saturdays at opposite ends of the town. You'll find the Bath Bus Station Fruiterers in Kingsmead Square. They have a range of seasonal English fruits and veggies, and sometimes a variety of exotic

>TOURIST

produce like mooli and plantain. Over on New Orchard Street, just outside the Marks & Spencers, you'll find Jimmy Deane's fruit and veg stall. You'll often be able to pick up a bowl of your favourite fruit or vegetable for £1 and it's quite fun just to hear the shouts of "Avocados! Pound a bowl! Pound a bowl!".

If you're from overseas and after a few home comforts, then you're in luck! Bath city centre has a few international supermarkets with a variety of products from around the world. They may not always be the cheapest place to shop, but at least you'll be able to ward off homesickness for a bit! Perfecto Market stocks goods from 59 different countries and is fascinating just for a browse! For Asian foods, head over to Hondo Supermarket, Friends Forever or Smile Oriental Market, where you'll find a range of Chinese, Thai, Japanese and Korean foods. These places are great for stocking up on snacks! You'll even be able to get hold of American sweets and cereals at Kingdom of Sweets, if you need to satisfy your sweet tooth.

For really fresh, high-quality local produce, you'll need to head out of the city centre. Newton Farm Shop over in Newton St Loe and Flourish Foodhall & Kitchen both have lovely cafés, so you'll be able to shop and then enjoy a tasty meal before you head back to Bath. If you're a cheese lover, you can't visit Bath without stopping by the Bath Soft Cheese Co. in Kelston. You'll also be able to watch the cheese being made, while you linger over a coffee in the lovely café.

## 35. BEST TIMES TO VISIT

With English weather having a reputation for being a little temperamental, you could be forgiven for wondering when is the best time of year to visit little old Bath. The truth is that there isn't really a bad time of year to visit us here in Bath!

If you come in the spring or autumn, the weather is relatively mild. Think crisp, clear days and (generally) blue skies. You may be subject to some of the infamous English rain (although it's nothing that a raincoat, umbrella and wellies won't take care of, if you're planning some outdoor activities). It also tends to be a little less busy in Bath for tourists during these seasons, but not to worry, there's still plenty to do and see!

Bath locals know that summer is peak tourist season. You'll often find locals avoiding the hustle and bustle of the city centre during these months. However, if you're looking for a dry, warm (dare we say, hot!) time of year to visit the city, then the summer months are the way to go.

When it comes to the winter months, weather-wise, Bath can get a little rainy and also fairly cold

>TOURIST

with temperatures hitting lows of 37ºF (3ºC). We occasionally get flurries of snow then, too. However, winter is still a great time of year to visit, even if it's purely to check out the festivities of the Bath Christmas Market!

If you're really not into crowds, there are a few days on the Bath events calendar that are worth taking note of. Rugby days draw crowds in for most of the afternoon and you'll find that there's more traffic, parking is trickier and bars and restaurants can be full. Check the Bath Rugby website if you're keen to avoid match days. Bath is also home to over 20,000 students, so you can imagine how many extra people are in the city on university open days, graduation days and when the students move in or out of their accommodation. Check Bath University and Bath Spa University websites if you're keen to avoid the worst of the crowds.

# 36. CURRENCY TO CARRY

If you've never visited the UK before, you may be forgiven for assuming we use the Euro here. However, even before the now infamous Brexit (where the UK left the European Union), we had our own currency.

To make any purchases in Bath, you'll need to be carrying pound sterling (GBP), AKA £s or the humble "quid". You'll find that Euros are not accepted anywhere in Bath. But never fear if you've forgotten to exchange your currency though, there are lots of places in the city centre where you can exchange your home currency for some pound notes. Nowadays, Bath has become more modern and like most cities in the UK, many shops and restaurants will accept a card or contactless payment, if you don't have cash to hand.

>TOURIST

# 37. YOU WON'T NEED A DICTIONARY!

If you've already got a good command of English, then you're pretty much good to go in Bath, language-wise. There is a real mix of accents here, partly due to its location in the South West, but also because of its proximity to London. Increasingly, you'll find Londoners are moving to Bath for the greenery and more relaxed lifestyle, whilst maintaining their careers in the English capital. The influx of international students has also helped Bath to become an amazing melting pot of cultures. The West Country accent can be a little thick, so if you do find yourself struggling to understand, don't be shy about asking the person to repeat themselves. Most people are friendly and understanding.

Basic greetings and manners are the same here as most parts of the UK. A simple "hello", "hi" or "good morning" is a typical way of greeting someone in a shop or restaurant. Likewise, when you leave, "goodbye" or "bye" are the norm, too. Bathonians, like many Brits, are known to be hot on manners, so ensure you say "please" and "thank you" to waiting staff and shop assistants.

American TV shows are popular across the UK, and so increasingly you'll find that American phrases are understood here. Perhaps more so with the younger generations. But here are a couple of differences that may catch out international visitors.

A "cellphone" is called a "mobile". We refer to bathrooms as "toilets" or "the loo". If someone tells you "That'll be three quid", they're telling you that your purchase costs £3. In a restaurant or café, we ask for the "bill" and do not call for the "check". A "cab" can also be referred to as a "taxi" and, surprisingly, Bath has even cottoned onto the "uber"!

But in all honesty, don't stress about it! We're a friendly bunch in Bath, and will do our best to help you!

# 38. DRESS FOR THE WEATHER

The No. 1 rule when you're packing your luggage to visit the UK is to dress for the weather! The UK weather is known to be changeable, so making sure you've got your bases covered is a must. Often it can be drizzling in the morning and clear blue skies in the afternoon. Packing light layers is a great idea as you can add or remove them, as and when you need to.

Keep in mind that much of the centre of Bath is outdoors. We don't have an indoor or covered shopping centre here. So that means if it rains, you're going to get wet! Make sure you've got a waterproof raincoat or umbrella handy at all times.

\>TOURIST

# 39. THESE BOOTS ARE MADE FOR WALKING

I'll admit, I'm a bit of a city girl, having grown up in London. So, I was not at all equipped or prepared for the sheer amount of rain we can get in Bath! But being out in the countryside, I have embraced country living and started taking walks along the Cotswold Way. Whilst the routes can be a little hilly, they're completely worth the effort for the stunning views of Bath, alone. They're also quite manageable, even for young children.

If you're planning to enjoy some of the lovely walks around Bath, make sure you bring a decent pair of hiking boots or wellies! A pair of trainers simply will not cut it, especially if it's been wet and the path gets slippery (trust me, I'm talking from personal experience here!).

## 40. WHERE TO GO FOR A HELPING HAND

Once in a while on your travels, you'll likely need some assistance. Whether it's for directions, lost or stolen property, or a recommendation for something, you'll need to call upon the help of someone knowledgeable.

If you've booked into a hotel, B&B or Airbnb, then your hotel concierge, receptionist or Airbnb host is very likely your first port of call. They should be able to help with things like recommendations, directions and even making restaurant reservations.

For something a little more serious, you can find the local police at the One Stop Shop on Manvers Street, which is near the railway station.

There are lots of social media groups full of locals, who will enthusiastically answer all of your questions. The power of social media is evident in the Lost & Found in Bath Facebook group, where you can write a post if you happen to have lost or dropped a belonging somewhere. For local events, the What's On In and Around Bath Facebook group is another great resource.

Sadly, the Bath Visitor Information Centre has been closed since Covid-19 hit, so you'll need to do your trip research in advance if you want to avoid

>TOURIST

stress once you arrive. There are some fantastic resources online to find out the latest opening dates and times for the main attractions, and of course, you've got this handy "Greater than a Tourist" guidebook. If you need help during your visit, then keep an eye out for the Bath BID Ambassadors, who will offer you a friendly smile and lots of advice.

# 41. DON'T FORGET THESE ESSENTIALS!

As well as the normal essentials, there are a few extra things that you'll want to pack when you come to Bath. We've already mentioned shoes, but they're worth mentioning again! Bring a comfortable pair of shoes or hiking boots. Most Bath attractions can be accessed on foot, plus Bath is quite a hilly part of the world. You're going to be doing plenty of walking just around the city centre, even if you're not planning on doing any hikes along the Bath Skyline or the Cotswold Way.

Chuck in a couple of tote bags in your luggage – they don't take up too much space and you'll thank me later. Like the rest of the UK, Bath is committed to reducing its environmental impact and shops now charge for plastic bags. Carrying a few tote bags around means you can shop knowing that you're not contributing to the increasing plastic problem.

Likewise, you may wish to carry around a reusable water bottle or coffee cup.

Don't forget your swimwear! That one may not be obvious since Bath is not a seaside town. However, it *is* a spa town! If you plan to visit the Thermae Bath Spa or any of the other wonderful hotel spas, you're going to need that swimwear.

If you're visiting Bath from overseas, make sure you bring enough travel adaptors. The UK runs on 230V supply voltage and 50Hz. Plugs have three rectangular pins arranged in a triangle formation. Most hotels will likely have a USB charge point, which is handy, but you may need extra adaptors or voltage converters or transformers to ensure you don't damage your appliances.

Last but not least, don't forget your camera! Or at least make sure you've got plenty of memory space on your phone. Bath is most famous for its beautiful Georgian architecture and pretty landscapes. I guarantee that you'll be snapping merrily away throughout your trip!

>TOURIST

## 42. TRAVEL SAFELY

On the whole, Bath is one of the safest cities in the UK. There aren't really any specific tips for the solo traveller in Bath, except apply common sense.

If you are travelling alone in Bath, then take the normal precautions. Make sure you know how to get back to your accommodation. Avoid having your valuables on display. Don't get ridiculously drunk. Stick to well lit streets and avoid walking along the river side or through a park, very late at night.

## 43. LGBTQ+ TRAVELLERS

Bath is a welcoming and inclusive city for all visitors. LGBTQ+ travellers are welcome everywhere. If you're after a LGBTQ+ specific night out, then try Mandalyns, which is Bath's popular gay bar.

The city hosts Bath Pride each year in February to celebrate the LGBTQ+ community. Various events and parades run during this time, such as drag bingo at the Komedia or Pride week at Moles.

# 44. PUBLIC HOLIDAYS

England's public holiday dates apply to Bath, but with the exception of Christmas, public holidays are unlikely to directly impact your trip (other than more visitors than normal!). The main museums, galleries and larger shops all tend to operate Sunday trading hours during public holidays, but are not usually fully closed. Independent shops, charity shops and smaller restaurants may choose to close during public holidays, so if you have your heart set on a particular shop, then phone ahead.

The exception to this rule of thumb is Christmas, when the vast majority of shops, restaurants and venues will be closed on Christmas Day. But be ready for Boxing Day (26th December), when everything opens up again for the Boxing Day sales!

>TOURIST

# 45. EASY TO WORK OUT SALES TAX AKA VAT

In some parts of the world, I find sales tax pretty confusing – the tax is added on at the till, or there are regional variances in the same country! I can't count the number of times that I've had to stand at the till counting out the coins in an unfamiliar currency because I couldn't work out how the sales tax worked! In the UK, sales tax is called Value Added Tax (VAT) and is (reasonably) straightforward from a consumer perspective.

Most food has no VAT added to it, unless it's considered non-essential. Think foods like crisps, confectionery, ice cream or alcoholic drinks. Non-essential food items are taxed at 20%, but the good news is the VAT is already added on the price tag, so what you see on the ticket is what you pay at the till (unless you've purchased a multibuy that qualifies for a discount, which is a whole different story).

In terms of clothing and souvenirs, you'll pay 20% VAT. Again, the price on the ticket usually already includes the VAT, so what you see is what you'll end up paying. The great news is that kids' clothing and toys, and all books are all exempt from VAT.

The bottom line is that you won't (usually) get a nasty surprise at the till, or need to get your phone out to work the amount of sales tax to add on, as all of the ticket prices reflect what you'll be charged at the end.

# 46. CLEAN AND FUNCTIONING PUBLIC TOILETS

Getting caught short (i.e. needing the bathroom) and not knowing where to find the nearest toilet can be a traveller's worst nightmare. So here's the lowdown on where to find a (reasonably) clean loo when you're out and about in Bath.

There are public toilets throughout Bath city centre in places like Charlotte Street Car Park, Monmouth Street, Southgate and the Podium/Waitrose. Some of the toilets are free to use, but the vast majority need a 20p coin to operate them. So make sure you keep some change with you! The last time I checked, the toilets didn't accept contactless payments.

If you're hanging out in one of Bath's many beautiful parks, you'll also be able to find public toilets there. Royal Victoria Park and Sydney Gardens both provide coin-operated toilets, so again, you'll need a 20p coin to use them.

Some of the larger shops in the city centre, like Marks and Spencers, provide toilets for their customers. Using one of these may be your best bet

>TOURIST

for a comfort break, if you're planning to buy something.

## 47. PARKING & EV CHARGE POINTS

Parking in Bath is not for the faint-hearted. First you've got to deal with the hill starts, then you've got to find a place to park AND make sure it's not only for residents.

Bath has worked for years on building out its Park & Ride infrastructure. There are three Park & Rides in the area: Newbridge, Lansdown and Odd Down. They take the headache out of finding somewhere to park in the city centre – just park your car and pay the bus fare into town. Bear in mind that lots and lots of people make use of the Park & Ride, so you may wish to time your return journey outside of peak times (like 6 pm, just after the shops close!).

If you do want to park closer to the city centre, then try Charlotte Street Car Park. This is Bath's long-stay car park, so you'll find the parking charge a little more reasonable than the short-stay car parks if you're planning to stay in the city centre for more than about four hours.

Some of Bath's parks, like Royal Victoria Park, provide free parking for an hour. You'll still need to get a ticket from the machine, but you won't need to pay unless you stay longer than the allotted hour.

Electric cars are gaining popularity around the UK, including in Bath. The good news is that the number of electric charge points is increasing all the time, so you'll be able to power up your car before the next leg of your journey. A few places that have electric charge points include Lansdown Park & Ride, Charlotte Street Car Park and Southgate Car Park. Download the Zap-Map app for up-to-date information about where you can find an EV charge point, how much it costs and whether it's occupied or even working!

# 48. SOCIAL MEDIA TO FOLLOW

Using social media is a useful way to get familiar with a place and plan your trip. There are some great Bath social media accounts to follow! Just type "Bath" into the search engine of your favourite social media platform and watch the hits come up! If you're feeling a bit overwhelmed, here are a few of my most useful social media accounts to follow.

For local news and traffic updates, try Bath Live (@bathlive). Visit Bath (@visitbath), and Total Guide to Bath (@totalguidetobath) are both great sources of inspiration for things to do once you get here.

>TOURIST

If food is your jam, then get onto following Bath Eats (@batheats), where you'll find some mouthwatering photos of some of the best restaurants Bath has to offer. Families may like to take a look at the Mums and More in Bath Facebook group, where the local parenting community are always keen to help one another with recommendations of things to do to entertain little ones.

## 49. SOME HOT TIPS FOR SOUVENIRS TO BRING HOME

Everyone loves to bring a souvenir home from their holidays – a little memento of your trip is a surefire way to brighten up your day.

If you've read our section on "The Great Sally Lunn vs Bath Bun Debate", then you'll know when it comes to souvenirs from Bath, you can't get more authentic than a box of light and delicious Sally Lunn Bath Bunns or a box of Bath Buns from the Bath Bun tea shoppe. If you didn't get a chance to taste test for yourself, then grab a box of both before you head home and extend your holiday by enjoying your very own taste test from home!

If you prefer a longer-lasting souvenir (because you can almost guarantee that those buns are going to be demolished as soon as you get home!), then have a wander around the Roman Baths' gift shop. A fun souvenir is a bottle of water from Bath's hot spring. The hot mineral waters were believed to have healing powers and were the original reason why the Romans built Aquae Sulis (AKA modern Bath), in the first place. If you've got kiddos in tow, then a Roman Baths guidebook probably won't go amiss and can double up as a useful resource for homework projects!

But if you're after something a little more unusual to remember your trip to Bath by, then take an afternoon wander around the historic Guildhall Market and stop by Gillards of Bath for some traditional English tea. The tea here is second to none, beautifully packaged, and sure to bring all your senses back to Bath, every time you make a cup!

>TOURIST

# THE FINAL WORD

# 50. SLOW DOWN!

If there's one thing I've learnt since moving to Bath is that life moves at a much slower pace here. And it's a wonderful lesson!

How many times do you find yourself rushing around and wishing you had a moment to pause for breath? In Bath, you can do just that. In fact, you should do just that – you're on holiday, after all!

Bathonians just seem to be more relaxed. You can pretty much walk everywhere you need to (just be sure to plan in the extra time to get to places), and it's so beautiful that you won't even be tempted to stare at your phone while you walk. Take a stroll through Royal Victoria Park or along the River Avon to get around and you're going to be surrounded by Mother Nature. Even meandering through the city centre, you need to take a look skywards and appreciate the wonderful buildings our ancestors have left us.

*Photo 10: Beside the River Avon, Bath*

And when you're tired of walking around, go and sit in one of Bath's many cafés. Sit inside with a book and enjoy the view. Sit outside and do some people-watching. You're not wasting time. Just breathe it in and enjoy the sights. You're here. It's Bath.

>TOURIST

# TOP REASONS TO BOOK THIS TRIP

**Architecture**: Beautifully preserved architecture from many historical periods, sit alongside modern buildings to make a truly unique city.

**Views**: Treat yourself to the stunning panoramic views that surround Bath. It's simply the English countryside at its best.

**Relax**: Bath is known as a spa town, and boasts the UK's only thermal hot springs. So slow down and relax at any of the city's beautiful spas, parks, or cafés.

>TOURIST

# LIST OF PHOTO SOURCES

*Photo 1: Suggestion for Cover Photo. View of Kelston Round Hill in January. Source: Sami Cheung, January 2022*

*Photo 2: The Great Bath, Roman Baths. Source: Sami Cheung, February 2019*

*Photo 3: Photo 3: Bath Abbey. Source: Richie Cheung, January 2014. Reproduced with permission*

*Photo 4: Enjoying the View from the Hare and Hound over Brunch. Source: Sami Cheung, December 2020*

*Photo 5: Taking an autumn walk along the Cotswold Way. Source: Sami Cheung, September 2022*

*Photo 6: In the Great Dell, Royal Victoria Park. Source: Sami Cheung, December 2020*

*Photo 7: Hot air balloon leaving Royal Victoria Park. Source: Sami Cheung, June 2021*

*Photo 8: The Royal Crescent, Bath. Source: Sami Cheung, July 2015*

*Photo 9: Pulteney Weir at Dusk. Source: Sami Cheung, September 2021*

*Photo 10: Beside the River Avon, Bath. Source: Sami Cheung, August 2021*

>TOURIST

# PACKING AND PLANNING TIPS

### A Week before Leaving

- Arrange for someone to take care of pets and water plants.
- Email and Print important Documents.
- Get Visa and vaccines if needed.
- Check for travel warnings.
- Stop mail and newspaper.
- Notify Credit Card companies where you are going.
- Passports and photo identification is up to date.
- Pay bills.
- Copy important items and download travel Apps.
- Start collecting small bills for tips.
- Have post office hold mail while you are away.
- Check weather for the week.
- Car inspected, oil is changed, and tires have the correct pressure.
- Check airline luggage restrictions.
- Download Apps needed for your trip.

## Right Before Leaving

- Contact bank and credit cards to tell them your location.
- Clean out refrigerator.
- Empty garbage cans.
- Lock windows.
- Make sure you have the proper identification with you.
- Bring cash for tips.
- Remember travel documents.
- Lock door behind you.
- Remember wallet.
- Unplug items in house and pack chargers.
- Change your thermostat settings.
- Charge electronics, and prepare camera memory cards.

\>TOURIST

# READ OTHER GREATER THAN A TOURIST BOOKS

*Greater Than a Tourist- California: 50 Travel Tips from Locals*

*Greater Than a Tourist- Salem Massachusetts USA 50 Travel Tips from a Local by Danielle Lasher*

*Greater Than a Tourist United States: 50 Travel Tips from Locals*

*Greater Than a Tourist- St. Croix US Birgin Islands USA: 50 Travel Tips from a Local by Tracy Birdsall*

*Greater Than a Tourist- Montana: 50 Travel Tips from a Local by Laurie White*

*Children's Book: Charlie the Cavalier Travels the World by Lisa Rusczyk Ed. D.*

# > TOURIST

Follow us on Instagram for beautiful travel images:
http://Instagram.com/GreaterThanATourist

Follow *Greater Than a Tourist* on Amazon.

CZYKPublishing.com

# > TOURIST

At *Greater Than a Tourist*, we love to share travel tips with you. How did we do? What guidance do you have for how we can give you better advice for your next trip? Please send your feedback to CZYKPublishing@gmail.com as we continue to improve the series. We appreciate your constructive feedback. Thank you.

>TOURIST

## METRIC CONVERSIONS

### TEMPERATURE

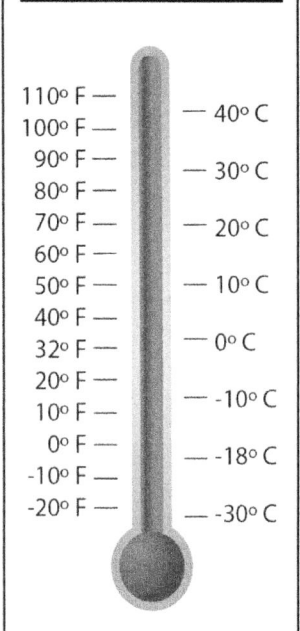

110° F — — 40° C
100° F —
90° F — — 30° C
80° F —
70° F — — 20° C
60° F —
50° F — — 10° C
40° F —
32° F — — 0° C
20° F —
10° F — — -10° C
0° F —
-10° F — — -18° C
-20° F —
— -30° C

*To convert F to C:*

Subtract 32, and then multiply by 5/9 or .5555.

*To Convert C to F:*
Multiply by 1.8 and then add 32.

*32F = 0C*

### LIQUID VOLUME

To Convert:................Multiply by
U.S. Gallons to Liters................. 3.8
U.S. Liters to Gallons .................26
Imperial Gallons to U.S. Gallons 1.2
Imperial Gallons to Liters....... 4.55
Liters to Imperial Gallons ........22
**1 Liter = .26 U.S. Gallon**
**1 U.S. Gallon = 3.8 Liters**

### DISTANCE

To convert ............Multiply by
Inches to Centimeters ....2.54
Centimeters to Inches ........39
Feet to Meters....................... .3
Meters to Feet ...................3.28
Yards to Meters ...................91
Meters to Yards ................1.09
Miles to Kilometers ..........1.61
Kilometers to Miles............ .62
**1 Mile = 1.6 km**
**1 km = .62 Miles**

### WEIGHT

1 Ounce = .28 Grams
1 Pound = .4555 Kilograms
1 Gram = .04 Ounce
1 Kilogram = 2.2 Pounds

>TOURIST

# TRAVEL QUESTIONS

- Do you bring presents home to family or friends after a vacation?
- Do you get motion sick?
- Do you have a favorite billboard?
- Do you know what to do if there is a flat tire?
- Do you like a sun roof open?
- Do you like to eat in the car?
- Do you like to wear sun glasses in the car?
- Do you like toppings on your ice cream?
- Do you use public bathrooms?
- Did you bring a cell phone and does it have power?
- Do you have a form of identification with you?
- Have you ever been pulled over by a cop?
- Have you ever given money to a stranger on a road trip?
- Have you ever taken a road trip with animals?
- Have you ever gone on a vacation alone?
- Have you ever run out of gas?

- If you could move to any place in the world, where would it be?
- If you could travel anywhere in the world, where would you travel?
- If you could travel in any vehicle, which one would it be?
- If you had three things to wish for from a magic genie, what would they be?
- If you have a driver's license, how many times did it take you to pass the test?
- What are you the most afraid of on vacation?
- What do you want to get away from the most when you are on vacation?
- What foods smell bad to you?
- What item do you bring on ever trip with you away from home?
- What makes you sleepy?
- What song would you love to hear on the radio when you're cruising on the highway?
- What travel job would you want the least?
- What will you miss most while you are away from home?
- What is something you always wanted to try?

## >TOURIST

- What is the best road side attraction that you ever saw?
- What is the farthest distance you ever biked?
- What is the farthest distance you ever walked?
- What is the weirdest thing you needed to buy while on vacation?
- What is your favorite candy?
- What is your favorite color car?
- What is your favorite family vacation?
- What is your favorite food?
- What is your favorite gas station drink or food?
- What is your favorite license plate design?
- What is your favorite restaurant?
- What is your favorite smell?
- What is your favorite song?
- What is your favorite sound that nature makes?
- What is your favorite thing to bring home from a vacation?
- What is your favorite vacation with friends?
- What is your favorite way to relax?
- Where is the farthest place you ever traveled in a car?

- Where is the farthest place you ever went North, South, East and West?
- Where is your favorite place in the world?
- Who is your favorite singer?
- Who taught you how to drive?
- Who will you miss the most while you are away?
- Who if the first person you will contact when you get to your destination?
- Who brought you on your first vacation?
- Who likes to travel the most in your life?
- Would you rather be hot or cold?
- Would you rather drive above, below, or at the speed limited?
- Would you rather drive on a highway or a back road?
- Would you rather go on a train or a boat?
- Would you rather go to the beach or the woods?

>TOURIST

# TRAVEL BUCKET LIST

1.

2.

3.

4.

5.

6.

7.

8.

9.

10.

>TOURIST

# NOTES